Introduction _____

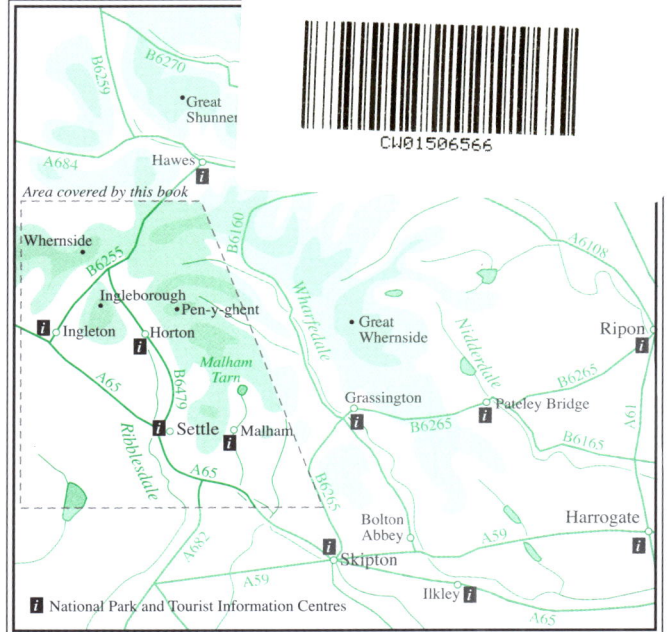

Area covered by this book

CW01506566

There are five major dales in the Yorkshire Dales: in the north, Swaledale and Wensleydale run from west to east; in the south, Ribblesdale, Wharfedale and Nidderdale run from north to south. The walks in this guide are in Ribblesdale, plus the hills and smaller dales to the west and east.

This is a rural area. The largest settlement is the little market town of Settle in Ribblesdale *(Walks 13,14,19)*, which is the main service centre for the district. The other settlements – Ingleton the largest – are little more than villages, and once the roads have climbed towards the heads of the dales there is little habitation. There is farming in the southern part of the area and up the floors of the dales, but beyond this the land is given over to rough grazing and grass moorland.

In some ways, the area provides routes which are typical of the walking to be found in upland areas throughout Britain.

Malham Cove (Walks 15,17)

What sets it apart is the impact of the local geology. The Dales are famous for their limestone landscapes, but no part of the Dales provides more dramatic limestone features than this south-western corner.

The picturesque little village of Malham is a good place to start. It is often busy, but the walking is superb. Nearby is Malham Cove *(15,17)*: a limestone amphitheatre with 250ft/76m white cliffs. The little Malham Beck bubbles out of the foot of the cliffs – an example of the underground watercourses typical of the area, while at the top of the cliffs there is an extensive limestone 'pavement': a mosaic of rock, broken like the mud on a dried lake bed, which can also be found on other walks in the guide *(see 2,4)*. Just east of Malham Cove is Gordale Scar *(16,17)*, a vast limestone gorge, while nearby the paths pass sink holes *(20)*, where becks disappear underground, and places like Aire Head *(22)*, where they reappear.

These subterranean watercourses create caves and potholes, which are another feature of the area. The largest is Gaping Gill *(6)*, which is large enough to hold York Minster. This is not accessible to casual walkers, but it is connected to Ingleborough Cave *(6)*, in the valley above the pretty village of Clapham, which is. Other large holes in the ground include Hull Pot, beneath Pen-y-ghent *(9)*, and Great Douk beneath Ingleborough *(4)*, but you will come across many smaller ones. Care should always be taken when approaching them: they are often much deeper than they look.

Another geological feature of the area is its numerous fine waterfalls. The famous Waterfalls Walk at Ingleton *(7)* is a good place to start, as it includes not only the elegant curtain of Thornton Force, but also the rapids of Baxenghyll Gorge. Elsewhere, routes pass Catrigg Force *(11)*, behind Stainforth (a brief diversion will also lead to Stainforth Force, on the Ribble) and many smaller falls.

A relic of the Ice Age in the Dales are the 'erratics': boulders carried from other parts of the country by glaciers and deposited in the landscape when the ice melted. You may come across these throughout the area, but notably at Twisleton *(2)* and Norber *(8)*.

The western side of this area is dominated by the Three Peaks: Whernside, Ingleborough and Pen-y-ghent. Their distinctive silhouettes will be familiar to anyone who has walked in the area, and they all present fine hill walking opportunities. Whernside *(1)* is the highest (2416ft/736m) and also the quietest – if you would rather climb without too much company, this is your best bet. Ingleborough *(3,4,5)* and Pen-y-ghent *(9)* are busier, but the walking is splendid and the views superb. There is a regular Three Peaks Race, where contestants have to make a circuit of the three hills.

All the routes in this guide fall within the boundaries of the Yorkshire Dales National Park – established in 1954 to conserve the natural and man-made beauty of the area. For more information on the National Park, visit **www.yorkshiredales.org.uk**, or one of the National Park Information Centres (in this area, at Malham).

It must be stressed that the walks chosen for this guide are only a fraction of the possible routes within the area. A brief study of the OS 1:25,000 maps of the area (strongly recommended for all walkers, as the illustration of the field boundaries is extremely useful) will show not only the network of rights of way and bridleways which criss-cross the area, but also the mass of 'Access Land' – mostly higher ground – which is now more generally open to walkers (though please observe any local signposting which contradicts the map). For more information, see inside back cover.

Chapel-le-Dale Church (Walk 2)

1 Whernside

A steep, testing circuit including the peak of the highest of the Three Peaks. Rough paths and superb views. Length: **8 miles/13km;** *Height Climbed:* **1,440ft/440m.**

O.S. Sheet OL2

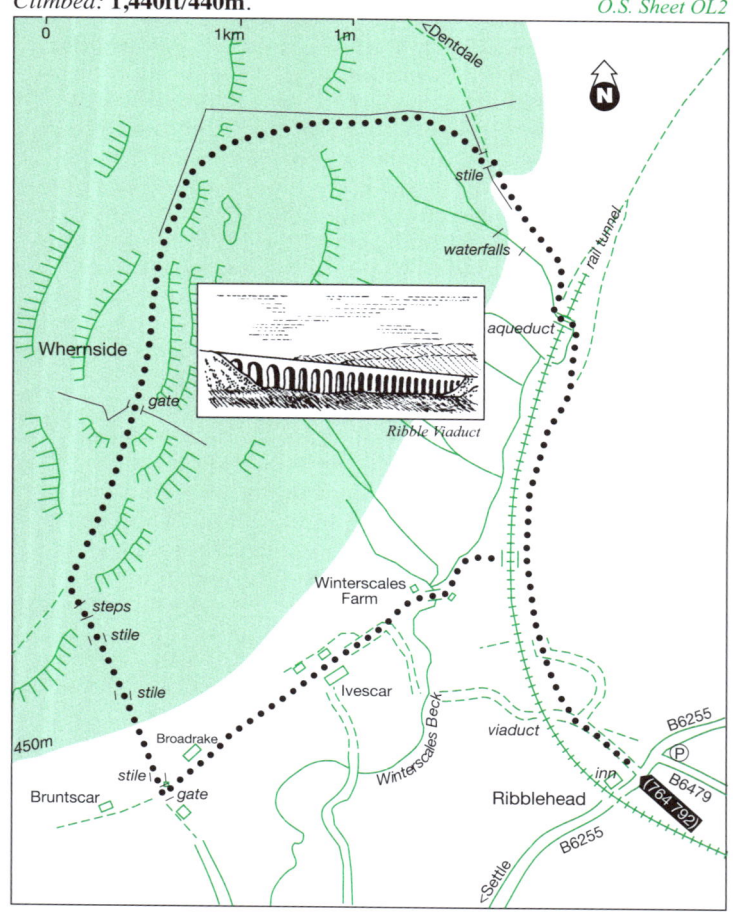

Ribble Viaduct

Whernside can be climbed from the north, but the obvious starting place is Ribblehead: 11 miles north of Settle at the junction of the B6479 and the B6255. The preferred parking is a short distance north of the Station Inn, by the road junction.

The clear track starts by the inn and runs parallel to the spectacular, 24-arch, Ribblehead rail viaduct (ignore paths to right and left), then continues, climbing, to the right of the railway line. Ignore further tracks running beneath the line to the left (the second of these is part of the return route) and continue to a split in the track from where a collection of stone walls is visible ahead.

Keep straight on here (ie, take the left-hand track), towards the walls. These are, in fact, a bridge and aqueduct crossing the railway. Cross over, noting the start of the Bleamoor Tunnel up to the right. A short distance beyond there is a signposted junction. Keep left here (Dentdale).

The climb becomes steeper now, with a fence to the left and fine waterfalls visible beyond. At a stile and signpost, cross the fence and follow the clear path which climbs – on stone steps in places – to the wall running along the north ridge of the hill. Turn left and follow the wall to the peak of Whernside. On a clear day, the views in all directions – Ingleborough (Walks 3,4,5), Pen-y-ghent (Walk 9), the Cumbrian Hills, Morecambe Bay – are quite superb.

Continue along the ridge beyond the peak. The key navigational question at this point is: when to turn off the ridge? Pass through a gate in a fence and continue. About half a mile/1km beyond there is a short, steep descent, beyond which the ridge continues as a plateau with the wall running along it. Just at the foot of the steep section, the main path sets off down the steep slope to the left. Take this.

Stone steps lead down to a wall crossed by stiles. Go over and continue, still on a clear path. Cross two further walls, the second with a barn just beyond it to the left. Just beyond this wall there is a gate to the left and a sign for Winterscales.

The route from this point is difficult to describe but easy enough to follow on the ground. Cross a field then pass in front of the buildings at Broadrake. Beyond, continue in the same direction across further fields (there are gates where required) to reach the farm buildings at Ivescar. Go through the farm and continue.

Just beyond Ivescar the track becomes a metalled road. Follow this until it heads off to the right. At this point keep straight on (Deepdale). The clear track passes to the right of Winterscales Farm, crosses a humpbacked bridge, then passes another house before reaching a gate at a point where two walls come together.

Go through this gate and continue, with Winterscales Beck to the left. The railway appears ahead with a tunnel running beneath it. Go through this and turn right to return to the start.

A fine circuit on rough, faint paths and quiet public roads, passing through extensive limestone pavements. A map and compass will be required on the hill section. Length: **7 miles/11km***; Height Climbed:* **up to 490ft/150m***. NB: Great care must be taken near the numerous potholes on this route.* *Possible extension of Walk 7.*

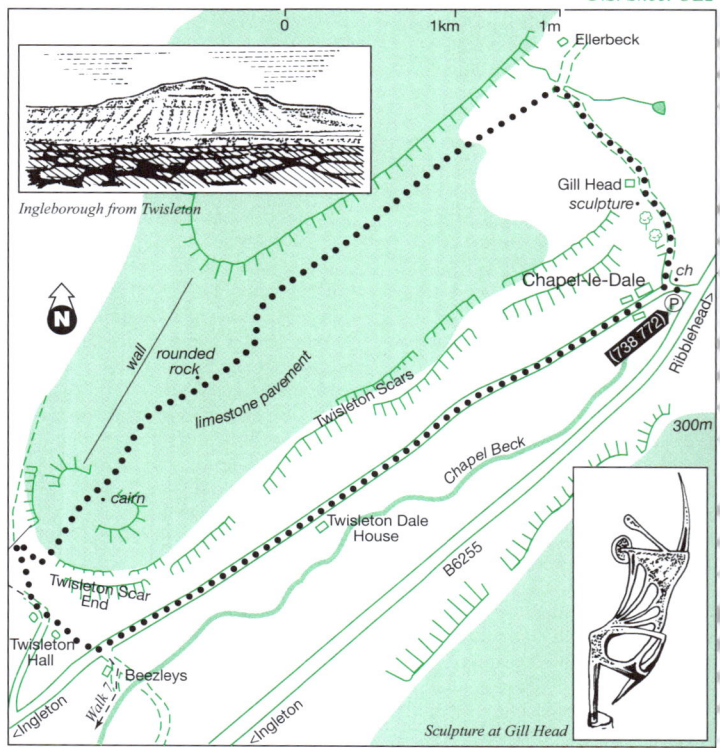

O.S. Sheet OL2

Ingleborough from Twisleton

Ellerbeck

Gill Head
sculpture

Chapel-le-Dale

ch

(738 772)

Ribblehead

wall
rounded rock

N

limestone pavement

Twisleton Scars

·cairn

Chapel Beck

Twisleton Dale House

B6255

Twisleton Scar End

Twisleton Hall

Beezleys

300m

∠Ingleton

Walk 7

∠Ingleton

Sculpture at Gill Head

Start this walk from the tiny village of Chapel-le-Dale. To reach it, drive four miles north from Ingleton on the B6255 and turn left onto a minor road. This road quickly drops to cross Chapel Beck. Just before the bridge there is a car park for the church to the left of the road (please avoid using this when the church is in use).

Walk across the bridge and past the church – a tiny, charming, 17th-century chapel – then turn right on a narrow metalled road leading uphill. When the road splits, keep to the right (Ellerbeck) and continue uphill. Note the sculpture to the left of the road shortly before Gill Head, and the fine view of Whernside ahead (Walk 1) once the walls have been left behind.

Climb up to the entrance to the farm at Ellerbeck, where there is a signposted junction. Go left here (Scar End), on a rough track at first. This becomes a faint footpath, but navigation remains easy at this stage: the route is virtually level and runs along the foot of a slope to the right. The moor stretches away to your left, with fine views beyond it across to Ingleborough (Walks 3,4 & 5).

The limestone pavement – the principal feature of this grassy plateau, which juts out like a ship's prow between two narrow valleys – starts to the left and the slope to the right gradually disappears. From now on there are numerous potholes amongst the clints (slabs) and grikes (fissures) of the pavement, and care must be taken to avoid accidents. Also, navigation becomes more difficult. There are paths across the moor and through the pavement, but it can be difficult to know which is the correct one; also, there are occasional blue-topped posts, but too few to navigate by.

When in doubt, keep heading in roughly the direction of the original path and watch out for a low, rounded rock which appears on the horizon ahead. A rough path passes to the left of it (it is only a metre or two in height), and from this point further landmarks are visible ahead: notably a triangular cairn with a 'V' in the horizon to its right. These features are on the edge of the plateau and the bridleway passes through the nick in the horizon.

Pass through the 'V' and drop down the slope beyond to reach another, smaller plateau. There are a number of paths through this area. When in doubt, stick to the main (ie, more frequently used) path. This drops down another slope, veering right to reach a junction at a wall, then doubles back to join the main track running along the foot of the slope. This part of the route is also part of Walk 7.

Turn left and follow the track past the buildings at Twisleton Hall (follow the signs for the Ingleton Waterfalls Walk) and on down to the public road. For this route, turn left along the road. There are walls to either side at first, but the road is quiet. After a short distance you cross a cattle grid and beyond that there are no walls or fences. This is useful for keeping out of the way of any traffic, but it does mean that you are likely to encounter grazing animals: keep out of their way wherever possible.

Follow this quiet road, with the dramatic Twisleton Scars up to the left, back to the start of the walk.

3 **Ingleborough from Ingleton /**
4 **Ingleborough from Chapel-le-Dale** —————— **A/A**

*Two of the most popular routes up this flat-topped hill, the definitive
landmark of the southern Dales (see also Walk 5).* **3)** *A long, gradual
ascent from the village of Ingleton, with one steep section near the peak.
Length:* **7 miles/11km** *(there and back); Height Climbed:* **1,900ft/580m.**
4) *A shorter, steeper climb from the north. Length:* **5 miles/8km** *(there
and back); Height Climbed:* **1,400ft/420m.** *Paths on both routes are
rough and wet in places. Views from the peak are superb, but navigation
on the summit plateau can be difficult in low cloud. Map and compass
are essential.*

O.S. Sheet OL2

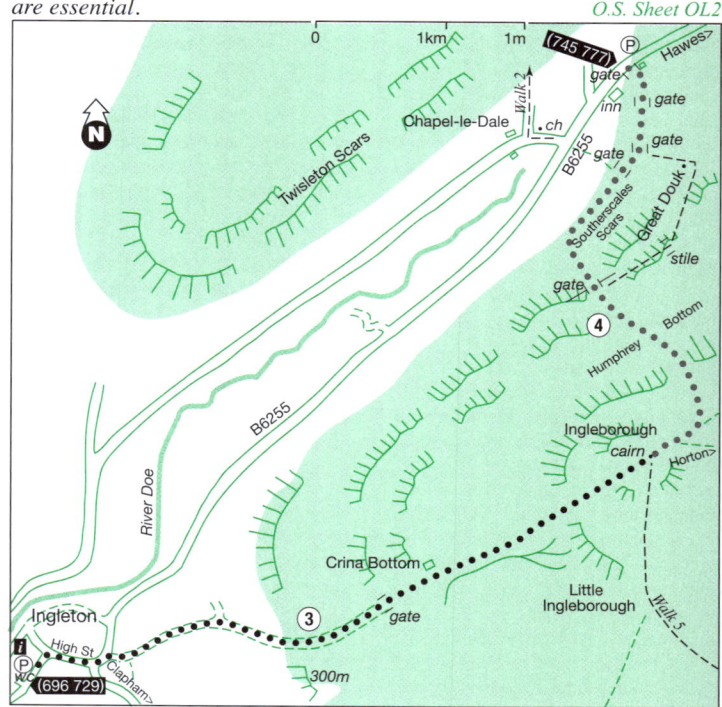

Walk 3) Start this walk from the village of Ingleton: nine miles west of Settle on the A65. Park in the village car park. Leave it by its eastern end (ie, walking away from the centre of the village) and turn left up the road (signposted for Hawes).

When the road splits, keep to the right (High St). At the next junction (when a road cuts right for Clapham), keep left. The road then climbs above the houses. Just beyond the last house turn right onto a clear track signposted for Ingleborough.

The track becomes a lane and continues to climb, with fine views to the west of Whernside (*see* Walk 1) and Twisleton Scars. When the lane ends, at a gate/stile, the peak of Ingleborough is visible ahead and the clear track continues through a charming open, grassy valley.

Past the building at Crina Bottom the path steepens again, becoming quite steep when climbing the bands of rock near the peak. The peak itself is a broad plateau, and you will need to walk around its outer edge to get the full extent of the superb views.

The best return is by the same route. There is a possible circuit, heading south from the top via Little Ingleborough and joining a quiet public road at Newby Cote, but the navigation on the lower slopes can be tricky (there is no clear path for much of the way) and the three miles of road walking to finish off is best avoided. If you do decide to try this route, add two miles/3km to the total length of the walk.

Walk 4) Drive north from Ingleton on the B6255 road for Hawes. After four miles the road passes the Old Hill Inn. A short way beyond there are two parking places to the left of the road.

Just by a small building (water treatment) there is a gate (entrance to the National Nature Reserve) and a sign for the path to Ingleborough. Start walking along a clear track, which leads to a gate in a wall. There is no clear path through the field beyond: continue in the same direction, aiming almost directly for the peak of the hill.

Beyond the next gate there is a junction of paths. Keep straight on. Beyond the third gate the path becomes clearer again; passing beneath the dramatic limestone ridge of Southerscales Scars then turning left and continuing between fine limestone pavements.

The path reaches a gate in a wall running across the slope. Beyond this the route is in little doubt: crossing a marshy area on a man-made path, then climbing steeply from Humphrey Bottom onto the ridge of the hill. Pass through a pedestrian gate and continue climbing south-west to reach the broad top of the hill.

There are possible alternative returns via Park Fell, but for this walk return by the same route. If you turn right above the transverse wall, a rough path marked by red posts ('Limestone Walk') will lead you back to the original path via the dramatic Great Douk pothole (*see* map).

5 Ingleborough from Clapham /
6 Ingleborough Cave & Gaping Gill _____ A/B

O.S. Sheet OL2

Two linked routes which both pass the entrances to Ingleborough Cave (open to the public, guided tours) and Gaping Gill (potholers only, except for special events). A small fee is due for access to the walk, plus a separate fee for access to the cave. **5)** *An ascent of the famous peak. The paths are clear, but navigation may be required on the surface plateau in low cloud. Map and compass essential. Length:* **8¹/₂ miles/14km** *(there and back); Height Climbed:* **1,850ft/ 560m.* **6)** *A pleasant circuit through a valley with woodland and a lake, plus a climb onto the moor to reach Gaping Gill. Some navigation required on the optional return route. The path to the cave is low-level, but the rest of the walk requires sturdy footwear. Length:* **5¹/₂ miles/9km*; *Height Climbed:* **820ft/250m**.

NB: Great care must be taken with children and animals when near pothole entrances.

Trow Gill

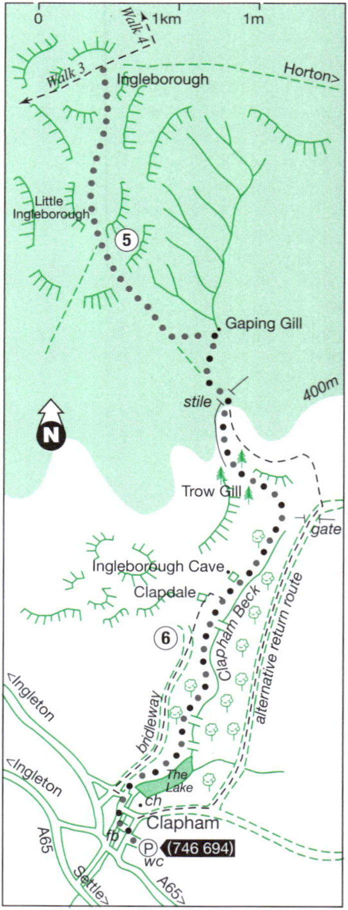

Start these routes from the village of Clapham: five miles north-west of Settle on the A65.

Walks 5 & 6) Park in the National Park car park in the village. At the entrance there is a sign for Ingleborough Cave. Go right for a short distance then cross Clapham Beck at the footbridge. Turn right at the far end and keep straight on to reach the entrance to the Nature Trail, where there is a machine for buying your ticket. (For an alternative start, along a bridleway, *see* map.)

The start of the route is straight-forward: up the side of The Lake then on up the wooded valley to reach the entrance to Ingleborough Cave (1½ miles/2.5km from the centre of the village). There is a ticket and refreshment kiosk at the entrance. The cave is vast, and is part of an even larger complex of caves and potholes spreading northwards (it is connected to Gaping Gill). The tour of the passages, with their stalactites and stalagmites, takes about 50 minutes.

Beyond the cave, a clear path continues up the valley, eventually swinging left to reach a gate. Continue beyond, with a wall to the left, towards the Gothic ravine of Trow Gill: its steep cliff sides topped by larch and pine.

Walk through the ravine, scramble up the rocky funnel at its head, and continue on a rough path through a grassy valley, with a wall to the left. Watch for the second stile crossing the wall. At this point a path heads up and back to the right. Take note

of this (it is the start of the optional return route), but, for now, cross the stile and continue. After a short distance the clear path splits. Go right and, in a short distance, the impressive entrance to Gaping Gill is reached. Take great care here: the rocks can be slippy and there is a vertical drop of 110m into the massive chamber below.

Walk 5) To continue the ascent of Ingleborough – visible ahead – take the linking path between Gaping Gill and the path which went left at the previous junction. The path is clear and the route obvious: straight up to Little Ingleborough then north up the ridge to the summit plateau. Return by the same route.

Walk 6) It is easiest to return by the same route, but if you wish an alternative: return to the stile over the wall and, on the far side, take the path previously noted.

The path rises gently at first, then runs level. A view of Thwaite Scars opens up ahead and a rough path heads off to the right. Ignore that and continue. From this point the path becomes fainter and navigation more difficult. If you continue in roughly the same direction, you should drop into a small dry valley then climb the other side on a track used by vehicles. This leads to a wall on the right in which there are two gates.

Go through the left-hand gate to enter an old lane. Follow this down the valley and take the track signposted for Clapham at the junction to return to the start.

A classic Dales walk: a circuit, largely on well-made paths, through two narrow, wooded valleys containing splendid waterfalls. The paths are steep in places and care must be taken by the falls. Length: **4¹/₂ miles/ 7km**; *Height Climbed:* **500ft/155m**. **NB:** There is a fee for this walk. Possible link with Walk 2.

O.S. Sheet OL2

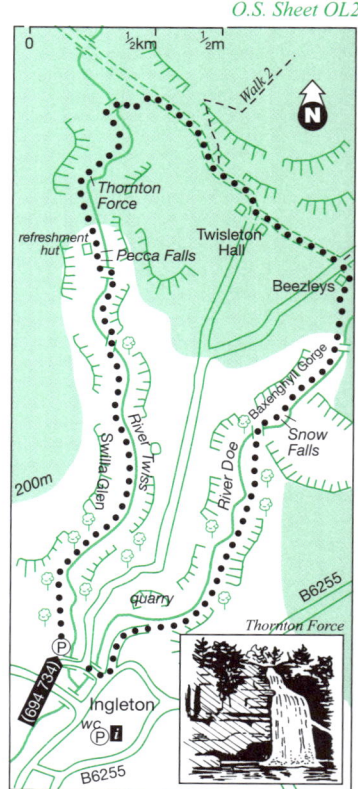

This splendid walk follows the narrow valleys of the Rivers Twiss and Doe, which converge at the village of Ingleton: nine miles west of Settle on the A65. There is a car park at the start of the walk, signposted from the centre of the village.

The route is well signposted and never in doubt. It starts by following the narrow Swilla Glen (River Twiss), with its broad-leaved woodland and limestone cliffs, before climbing past the Pecca Falls (and the refreshment hut above them) to reach the splendid Thornton Force with its wide curtain of water.

Above the falls the path enters an area of grassland with a footbridge visible ahead. Cross the bridge and climb up to join a lane. Turn right along this (signposted), passing behind Twisleton Hall and noting the fine view of Ingleborough ahead (*see* Walks 3,4 & 5).

Drop down to the public road and cross over to reach Beezleys farm. Turn right in front of the farm then go through a gate at the end of the buildings. The path from here is well maintained and easy to follow: passing the dramatic Baxenghyll Gorge and Snow Falls in this narrow, oak-filled valley.

The path eventually joins the public road on the outskirts of Ingleton.

A short, moderate climb on public road, track and rough footpaths to a group of geological features and a fine viewpoint. Length: **3 miles/5km;** *Height Climbed:* **500ft/150m.**

O.S. Sheet OL2

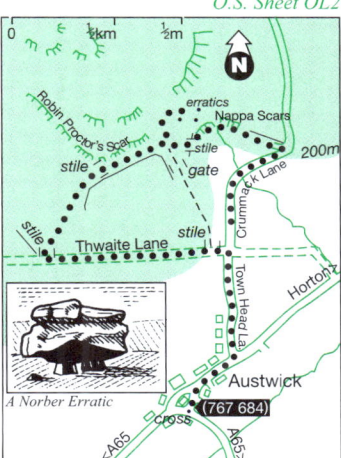

A Norber Erratic

Start from the little village of Austwick – just north of the A65, six miles east of Ingleton. There is no car park: park by the roadside.

From the crossroads in the centre of the village, walk along the road for Horton. Near the end of the village, turn left up Town Head Lane.

Follow the road out of the houses and continue. (The road is quiet but narrow: listen out for traffic). ¹/₃ mile/0.5km up the lane there is a junction, with vehicle tracks heading off to left and right (Thwaite Lane). Turn left.

Almost immediately there is a gate/stile to the right. This is a short cut to the erratics (*see* map). For the longer route, continue along the lane, noting the cliffs of Robin Proctor's Scar to the right.

Watch for a sign for Norber to the right of the track. Cross a stile over the wall and walk across the field to the corner formed by the wall to the right, then continue across the slope with this wall to your right.

Cross a stile over a wall across the route and continue until the wall bends away to the right. At this point a rough footpath climbs up to a signposted junction on a low, rocky ridge. Go left (Norber) and climb through a shallow, scree-filled gully. Go straight on for a short distance above the gully, then swing right (there is a large cairn ahead of you at this point)

to reach the erratics.

Erratics are boulders carried many miles by glaciers in the last Ice Age. In this case, the boulders are of harder rock than the native limestone, which in places has eroded beneath them, leaving them standing on 'stalks'.

Explore the erratics then return to the signposted junction. Go left (Crummack) to reach a wall. Climb up by this short way then cross a stile. Continue with a wall to the right to a wooded cliff (Nappa Scars). Go through the gap at the end of the wall and follow a pleasant path across the face of the cliff and on down to the public road.

Turn right to return to Austwick.

A steep, rough circuit which scrambles to the peak of the lowest of the famous Three Peaks. Length: **6 miles/9.5km**; *Height Climbed:* **1,500ft/ 460m**. *Paths rough but generally clear.*

O.S. Sheet OL2

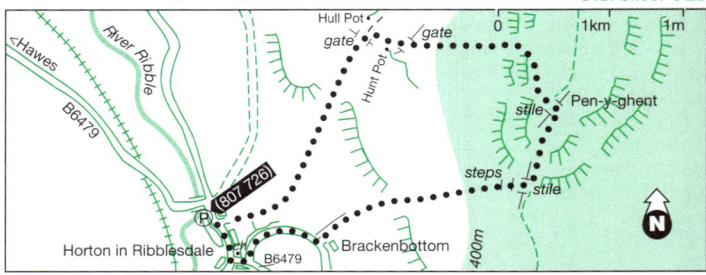

Start this walk from the National Park car park in Horton in Ribblesdale, five miles north of Settle on the B6479.

Walk back in the direction of Settle, passing the church and swinging left across the bridge. Immediately beyond the bridge turn left on a minor road and follow this out of the village and uphill to the buildings at Brackenbottom.

The path to the ridge is clear from here: just keep the wall to your left to find the gates and stiles in the transverse walls. On the final climb to the wall along the ridge there is a flight of stone steps. Cross the stile over the wall and turn left, up the ridge.

At first there are more steps, then some light scrambling over a limestone section, before you reach the trig point at the summit. The views are superb.

Cross one of the stiles over the wall to your left. Beyond this you will be on the footpath signposted for Horton. Follow this clear, rough path, which angles down the slope towards the foot of the little cliffs of Pen-y-ghent Side, then swings left down a gentler slope.

A wall crosses the way. A diversion to the left a little beyond this will lead to the sight of a beck disappearing into Hunt Pot (be *very* careful near the edge, this is very deep). Return to the path and continue to another wall. 100m beyond this there is a further junction. The path to Horton follows the lane which opens to the left, but before taking it make a brief detour to the right to see the spectacular Hull Pot: a 100m gash in the moor, with sheer sides dropping to a shingle floor. If you visit in winter, you may be lucky enough to see the waterfall entering the Pot from the north.

The lane runs without complications down to Horton. As it approaches the houses it splits: keep right to return to the start.

A short, low-level circuit by the River Ribble. Length: **2¹/2 miles/4km**;
Height Climbed: negligible.

O.S. Sheet OL2

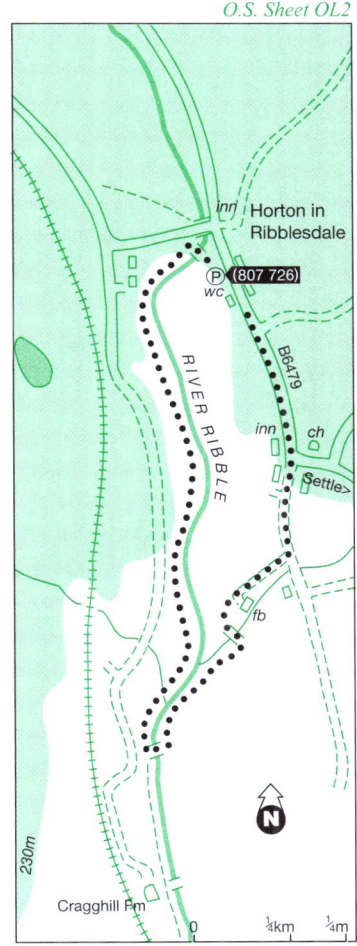

Horton in Ribblesdale is a small, straggling village, five miles north of Settle on the B6479. It is best known as the start point for strenuous walks up Pen-y-ghent (*see* Walk 9) and Ingleborough, but this is a less taxing excursion.

Park in the National Park car park at the north end of the village. Walk north past the toilet block and cross the footbridge over the river. At the far end drop down a flight of steps, turn left, and follow the river bank (there is no path at this point).

Follow the river for about a mile/1.5km, until Cragghill Farm becomes visible ahead and there is a well-maintained footbridge to your left. Climb the steps onto the bridge and cross the river.

At the far end turn left, go through a gate and follow the edge of a field with trees along it. The field edge swings away from the river beside a tributary beck. Looking ahead there is a footbridge over the beck with a house visible beyond it.

Cross the footbridge and turn right, by the beck, to join the access track to the house. Follow this away from the house, between fields at first and thrn straight on through houses, to return to the main road through Horton, just opposite the church.

When the track joins the main road turn left to return to the start.

Walks Malham & The Three Peaks

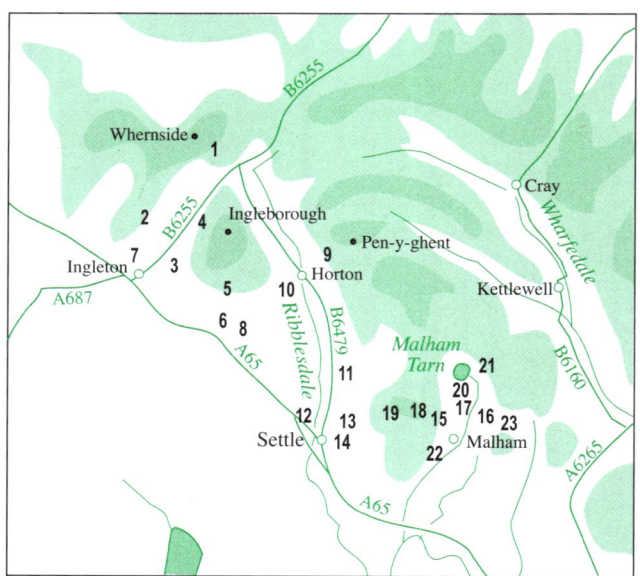

Grades

A ...... Full walking equipment required

B ...... Strong walking footwear and waterproof clothing required

C ...... Comfortable walking footwear recommended

— www.pocketwalks.com —

Published by: Hallewell Publications, Scotland
Printed by: J Thomson Printers, Glasgow

While every care has been taken in the preparation of
this guide, the publishers cannot accept responsibility
for any loss, damage or injury resulting from its use.

Walks Malham & The Three Peaks

A short, steep circuit passing a fine waterfall. Some navigation needed on the return. Length: **2 miles/3km**; *Height Climbed: up to* **490ft/150m.**

O.S. Sheet OL2

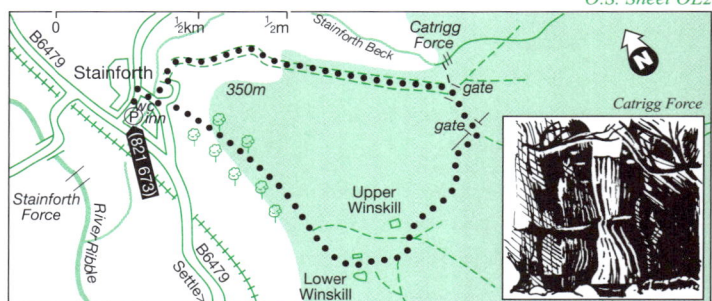

Stainforth is a small village two miles north of Settle on the B6479. Park in the National Park car park just off the main road and walk into the village. At the junction turn right, across the bridge, then immediately left to follow a path by Stainforth Beck. When this rejoins the road turn left, past a small green, then right, uphill.

It is a steep, pleasant climb to the end of the lane, where the diversion to Catrigg Force is signposted to the left. It is difficult to see the fall from above, but a path winds round to the bottom of the fall for the best view.

Return to the end of the lane. There are three gates here: go through the right-hand one then bend right, uphill, towards a gate in a wall. Beyond this go right, off the track, on the path signposted for Winskill.

The path becomes a track and enters a lane which continues down to a junction by Upper Winskill. Go ahead-left here, down the access road, and continue down to the buildings at Lower Winskill.

Walk between the house and the barn to reach a gate. Go through this, then half-right across a small paddock to reach a stile over a wall. Climb straight up the slope beyond then right (yellow arrow) on a rough, clear path.

A wall comes in from the right with a gate/stile. Continue along the narrow field beyond, dropping gently to the line of the fence to the left. At the end of the field cross a stile to enter an area of woodland.

A flight of stone steps leads down and across the steep wood (there are crags to the left initially, be careful). There is a kissing-gate leading into a field at the bottom. Go through this and continue along the top of the field. At the end there is a gate into a narrow field. Ignore the gate directly opposite and head half-left to enter a lane leading back into the village.

*A short, steep climb, through woodland and over the open hill, to a
fine viewpoint. If you have children or animals, please note that care
should be taken both by the edge of the scar and around the quarry edge.
Length:* **2-3 miles/3-5km***; Height Climbed:* **430ft/130m***.*

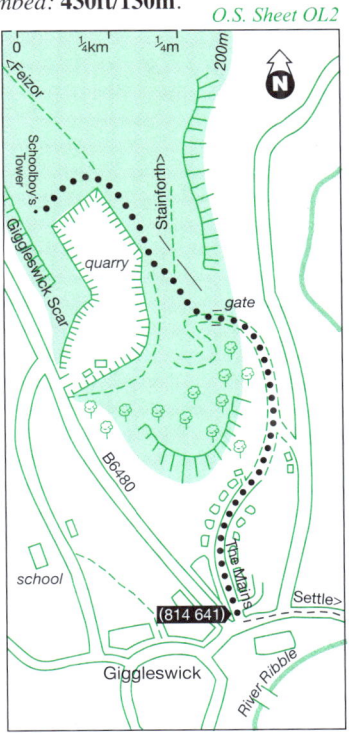

O.S. Sheet OL2

Giggleswick is the picturesque little
village on the far side of the River
Ribble from Settle. Giggleswick Scar
is the steep, wooded slope above the
B6480 to the north of the village.
This walk climbs the back of this
hill, passing the large (and active)
Giggleswick Quarry on the way. **NB:**
there may be blasting in the quarry;
please take note of all warnings dis-
played along the route.

   Parking is limited in Giggleswick,
and it may be easiest to park in Settle
and walk across the bridge. Once in
the village, look for the road called
'The Mains' (heading right, if you are
coming from Settle). Follow this road
to its conclusion then continue on a
clear track across the slope of the hill.

   Another track joins from the right
and you continue: entering an area
of broad-leaved woodland and then
climbing to a gate at the top of the
trees. Beyond the gate, leave the
track immediately on a rough, clear
path to the right.

   The path splits, with the right-hand
path passing through a wall. Ignore
this and continue climbing the hill,
eventually reaching the quarry's
boundary fence which runs along the
ridge. Turn right along this, bending
left when it does to reach the large
cairn known as Schoolboys' Tower.

There are splendid views from here.
A study of the OS map will show
possible extensions to Stainforth or
Feizor, but for this walk return by the
same route.

13 Victoria Cave Loop _____ B

A moderate but complicated circuit, including some climbing, leading through fields to caves in a rocky scar. Length: **4¹/₂ miles/7km**; Height Climbed: **850ft/260m**. *NB: great care should be taken by anyone approaching these caves. Rockfalls are not uncommon.* O.S. Sheet OL2

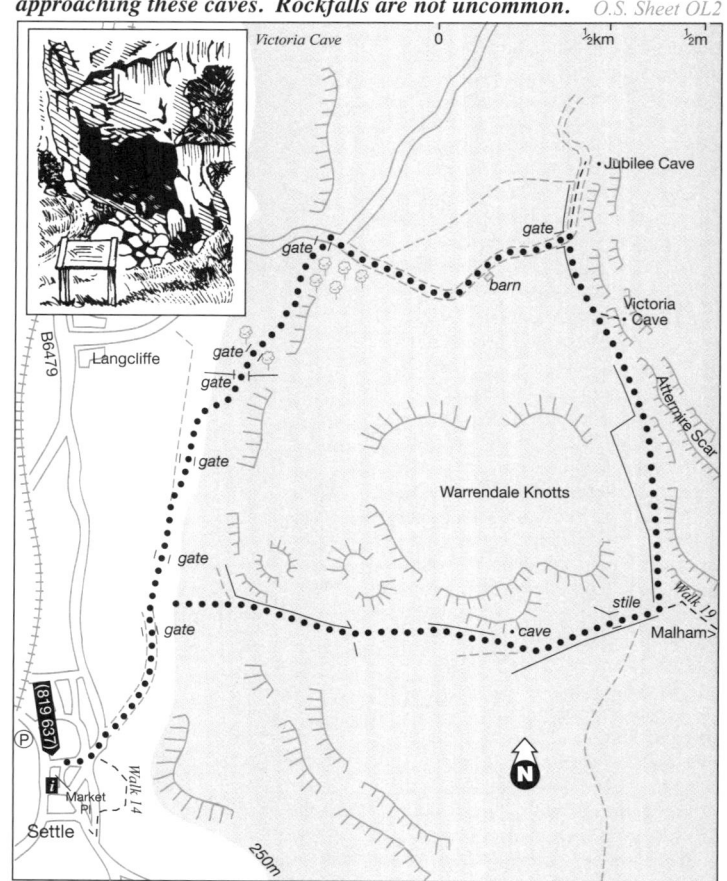

Park in Settle and walk to the Market Square. Walk up past the NatWest bank and on up Constitution Hill. When the road splits, go left (Bowskills Yard). The road swings left and quickly splits again.

A metalled road continues to the left, but for this route go right on a vehicle track signposted for Langcliffe. The track, between walls, is well maintained, and there are fine views over Settle, down to the left.

Go through a gate and continue with a wall to the left. After 100m there is a sign pointing to the right (Malham). This is the end of the return route, but for now keep straight on with the wall to the left. Pass through two further gates. After the second gate the wall on the left drops away and you should head half-right (there is no clear path through this field: aim to walk below a stand of trees, the tops of which are visible from the gate).

Pass through a gate at the near corner of the wood and continue with the trees to the right to reach a further gate. Beyond this, follow a clear, rough path which passes below a second copse, visible on the far side of the field. Swing right round the end of the trees to reach a gate leading onto the public road.

At the signposted junction beyond the gate go right (Settle Loop). The track climbs gently, passing an old barn, to reach a transverse wall running along beneath the line of the scars.

Go through the gate in the wall.

A brief detour to the left at this point leads to the small Jubilee Cave. Otherwise, turn right and walk along with the wall to your right. Watch for the start of the steep little path leading up to Victoria Cave. The cave has been extensively excavated and was found to contain animal bones dating back 130,000 years. (*NB: take great care if exploring the cave*.)

Return to the main path a continue by the wall. When the wall pulls away to the right keep straight on. After a short distance the wall returns and the path steepens and drops between rocky outcrops and scree with the wall to the right. At the foot of the slope go right (*NB: this is the point at which* Walk 19 *joins this route*) with a wall to the left. Cross a stile over a transverse wall and continue with a wall to the left and a dramatic rocky outcrop ahead and to the right. As you approach this a cave becomes visible.

Pass through a gap in a transverse wall. Immediately beyond this the path splits. Keep right, making a diversion to visit the cave then continuing with a wall to your right. The path passes through a pedestrian gate in a transverse wall and begins to descend, now with the quarry at Giggleswick visible across the valley (*see* Walk 12).

When the wall bends away to the right a faint path follows it. Ignore this and continue down the slope to rejoin the outward path at the point previously noted.

Turn left to return to Settle.

*A very short walk: a steep climb from the centre of Settle to a viewpoint at the top of a limestone crag. Length: **1 mile/1.5km**; Height Climbed: **165ft/50m**. Care should be taken with children and animals.*

O.S. Sheet OL.

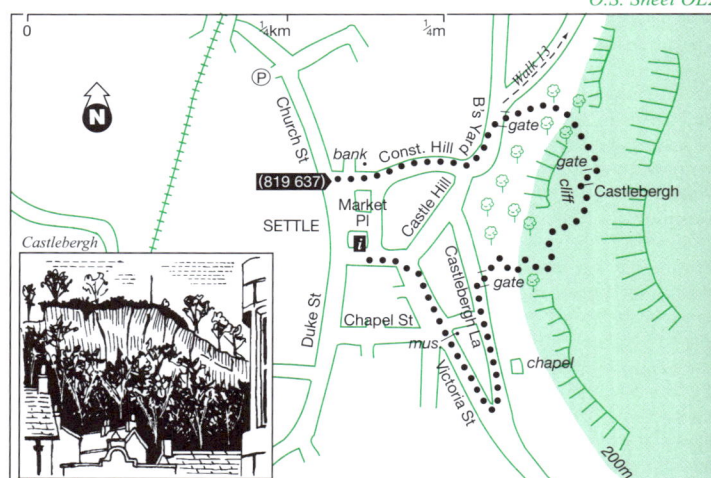

From the square in the centre of the fine old market town of Settle (from where Castlebergh and its flagpole are clearly visible), start walking as for Walk 13: past the NatWest Bank and on up Constitution Hill. When the road splits, go left (Bowskills Yard). Just before it splits again there is a large wooden gate to the right of the road.

Go through the gate and follow the clear path beyond: climbing through mature woodland, parallel to the wall to your left at the edge of the wood. When the wall swings right the path follows it, eventually passing through

a gate to reach the summit of the rock

The views from the top are splendid, but **be careful not to go too near the edge of the cliff**.

The path continues beyond then zig-zags back down to Settle (there are a number of paths exploring the slope below the crag).

The path ends at a gate leading on to Castlebergh Lane. Turn left along this. Just beyond the Methodist Chapel, turn right down Victoria St, passing the splendid 17th-century house (the Folly) which now houses the Museum of North Craven Life, to return to the start.

A short there-and-back walk on clear paths to the famous and spectacular limestone amphitheatre, with a possible extension up a long flight of steps to the top of the cliffs. This site can also be reached as part of the circuit described in Walk 17, which also passes Gordale Scar. Length: **2-3 miles/3-5km** *(there and back); Height Climbed: up to* **330ft/100m** *(to top of cliff).* **NB: Children and animals should be kept under close control near cliff-tops.**

O.S. Sheet OL2

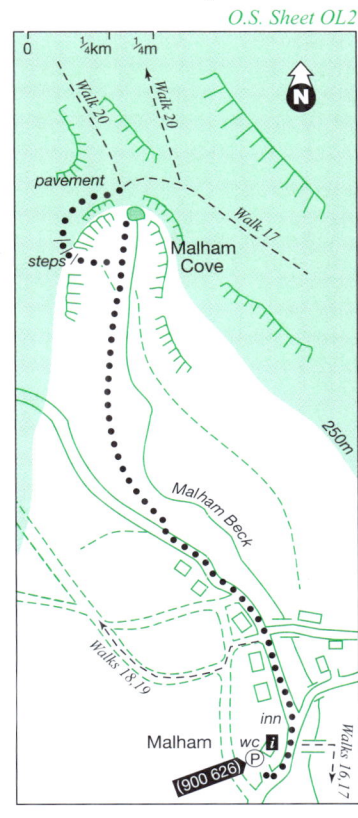

Start this straightforward and hugely popular walk from the National Park car park on the outskirts of Malham. Walk northwards, through the village, keeping to the left of Malham Beck.

Follow the road uphill and out of the village. Shortly beyond the last of the houses the Pennine Way cuts off to the right. Turn on to this clear path and follow it to Malham Cove, which soon comes into view.

A rough path leads up the side of the beck to the foot of the 250ft/75m white cliff at the point where the water, which once would have cascaded down the rock face, now bubbles up from the foot of the cliff into a large pool.

Retrace your steps to reach the start of the path which cuts off to the west; climbing a long flight of steps to reach the top of the cliffs. The views from the top are stunning (though be careful not to go too near the edge: the drop is sheer), but the main attraction of the climb is the extensive 'limestone pavement': an expanse of limestone slabs ('clints') divided by deep, narrow fissures ('grikes').

After exploring, return by the same route.

A short, there-and-back walk on clear paths to one of Malham's two famous geological features, passing a waterfall along the way. For possible extensions and circuits, see Walks 17 & 23. Length: **4 miles/ 6.5km** *(there and back); Height Climbed: up to* **165ft/50m**.

O.S. Sheet OL2

Start from the National Park car park on the outskirts of Malham and walk towards the centre of the picturesque village. Cross the first bridge over the beck (a stone footbridge with a metal handrail) and turn right on the far side (signposted for the Pennine Way and Janet's Foss).

Just beyond a kissing-gate there is a signposted junction. Go left here, passing a stone barn and climbing gently by the Gordale Beck on a well-made path into the ash woodland surrounding Janet's Foss – a pleasing waterfall.

Above the fall a gate leads on to the public road. Turn right along this (watch out for traffic on this short stretch). After a short distance there is a hump-backed bridge to the left of the road and the start of a signposted footpath (*see* Walk 17). Ignore this and continue along the road for a short distance to the next signposted path. Turn left onto this and follow it up the narrowing dale into the magnificent limestone gorge of Gordale Scar.

You will see people scrambling up the rocks at the head of the gorge, but this is not recommended for inexperienced walkers. For this route, double back along the same route. If you wish to extend the walk, *see* Walks 17 and 23.

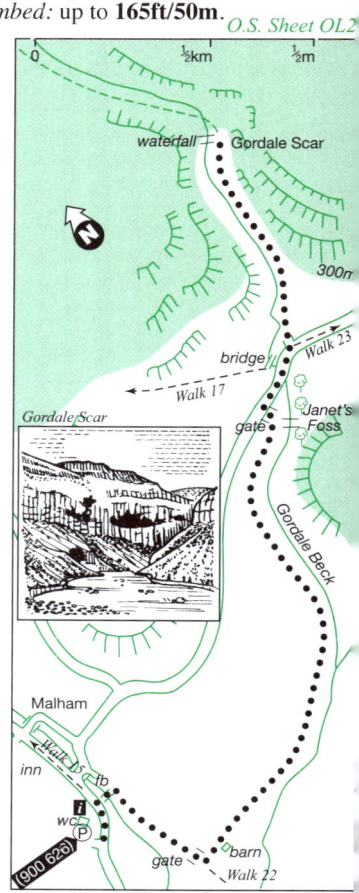

17 Gordale Scar & Malham Cove _____ B

A moderate circuit, largely on paths and across short grass but including a descent of a long flight of steps, passing the two great geological features north of Malham. Length: **4¹/₂ miles/7km**; *Height Climbed:* **430ft/130m**. *NB: Some care needed with children and animals near Malham Cove cliff-tops. Possible extension on Walk 20.*

O.S. Sheet OL2

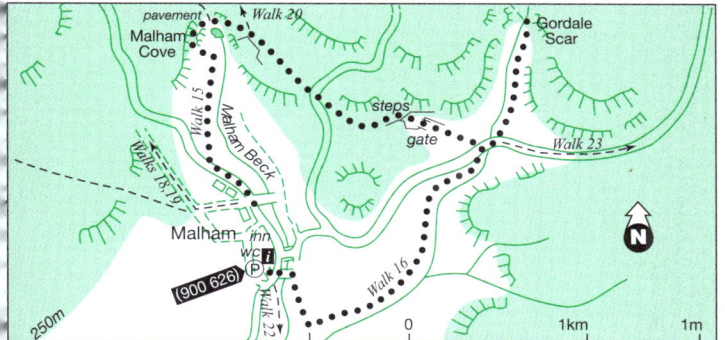

Start this walk as for the Gordale Scar route (Walk 16). Follow this route to the Scar and then back as far as the hump-backed bridge (Gordale Bridge) mentioned in the text.

From the bridge, take the path signposted for Malham Cove, which starts by climbing a field with a wall to the right. Pass through a gate and a clear path climbs to a flight of steps and a gate in the corner up to the right. Pass through this gate and continue, with the wall to the left and the open hill up to the right, to reach the public road.

Cross the road and continue through an area of rough grazing with bare limestone showing through the grass. The clear, rough path runs broadly parallel to a wall down to the left. After a short way the wall climbs sharply to join the path, runs beside it for a distance, then cuts away again. At this point there is a junction.

For the Malham Tarn walk (*see* Walk 20) go right. For this walk, keep to the left (signposted for Malham Cove) and drop down to a stile and a junction. Go straight on (Pennine Way) across the limestone pavement above Malham Cove.

At the far end of the cove, go through a kissing-gate and climb down the long flight of steps to reach the foot of the cliffs. After exploring the area, take the clear path down Malham Beck to join the pubic road and turn left to return to the start.

18 **Pikedaw** / 19 **Malham to Settle** ____________ **B/B**

18) *A short, steep circuit passing a viewpoint overlooking Malhamdale. Length:* **4½ miles/7km***; Height Climbed:* **985ft/300m**. **19)** *A lineal route linking the village of Malham with its nearby market town. Length:* **6 miles/9.5km** (one way)*; Height Climbed:* **985ft/300m (1,150ft/350m if** walked west to east). *It is possible to return by the same route, perhaps finishing along the route of Walk 18, but there is no direct public transport link between the two ends of the walk.*

O.S. Sheet OL2

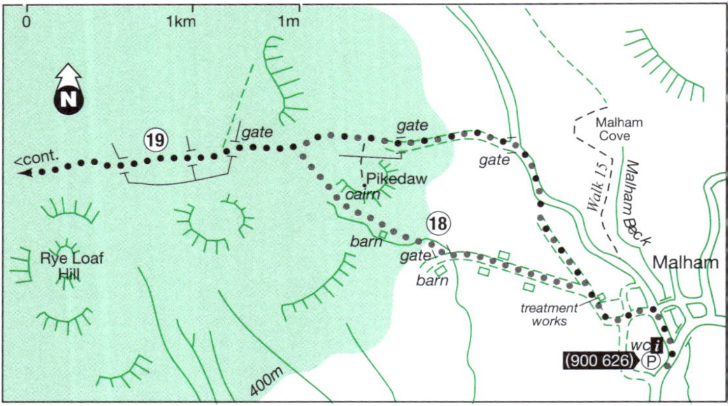

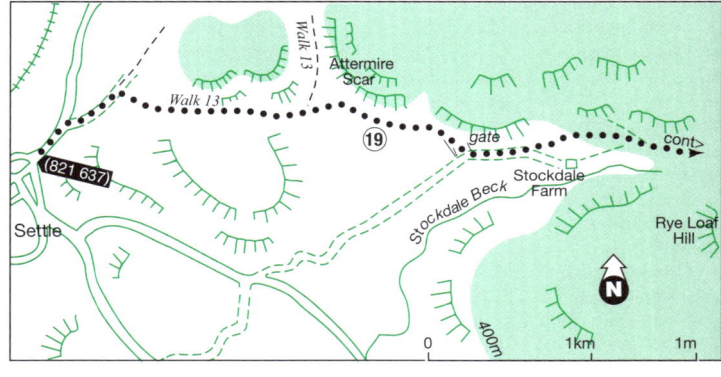

Walks 18 & 19) Start from the National Park car park on the edge of Malham. Leave the car park and walk up through the village. Pass the road junction in the village centre and continue up the left-hand side of Malham Beck. Opposite a sign for the Beck Hall B&B there is a sign, on the left, for a bridleway. Turn onto this.

Walk up between walls to a junction with a vehicle track and turn left. After 30m the track splits. Go right, uphill. Just beyond a water treatment works the track splits. Go right and follow the track up to the public road.

Turn left up the road and continue climbing, watching for a gate to the left and a sign for the bridleway to Settle. Turn left here.

Beyond the gate a clear, rough track winds gently uphill to reach a gate in a wall. Pass through this and continue. A cairn becomes visible, ahead and beyond the wall to the left. This is Pikedaw. Watch for a rough path heading off to the left to a gate in the wall. Make a brief diversion at this point to see the fine views of Malham and the surrounding hills from the cairn before returning to the main path.

Continue along the clear path until a three-way junction is reached, marked by a signpost.

Walk 18) To return to Malham from this point, turn left. The rough path runs flat at first, through a limestone pavement, then descends steeply into a small valley, eventually reaching a wall with a stile over it. Cross the stile and continue on the clear path down the valley.

Cross a stile to the left of the first barn in the valley and continue with the beck to your right. At the next wall, cross the beck then cross the field to a gate by the lower of two barns to join a lane. Turn left along this to return to the junction by the water treatment works, then retrace your steps to the start of the walk.

Walk 19) To continue the walk to Settle, carry on ahead along the clear path, climbing to a gate in a wall. Beyond the gate there is a junction. Go straight on (signposted for Stockdale Lane).

The clear track passes through two gates and begins to descend. Ahead, Stockdale Farm comes into view. The track drops down towards the farm (at a fork, ignore the track heading off to the right) but passes above and to the right of it, with a wall to the left.

Beyond the farm the track reaches the lane end, just by the farm entrance. Walk on down the road until, where it turns hard left, there is a gate to the right. Go through this and continue walking with the wall to the left (signposted for Settle).

Continue walking roughly parallel to the wall to the left, passing through transverse walls, until a gap opens up in the crags and scree (Attermire Scar) to the right. A wall drops downhill through this gap. This is the line taken by Walk 13. To complete this walk, carry on with the crags to the right and follow the instructions for Walk 13 from this point.

*This is a longer versions of Walk 17, which extends that route, across open country, to the little hill lake of Malham Tarn. Possible link with Walk 21. Length: **9¹/₂ miles/15km**; Height Climbed: **600ft/180m**.*

O.S. Sheet OL2

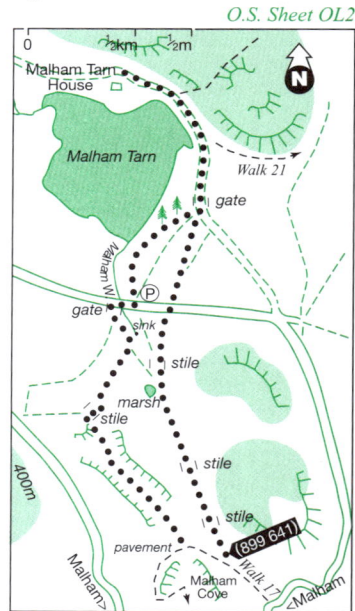

Start this walk following the route descriptions past Gordale Scar and onwards given in Walks 16 and 17. When the junction is reached by the corner of a wall (*see* Walk 17), go right. There is no signpost for the route, but a clear, grassy path leads to a stile over a wall, visible ahead.

Cross this and continue on the grassy path beyond, climbing to a further stile just short of the watershed. Beyond the watershed, the path drops to the right of an area of marsh and small pools, just beyond which there is a signposted junction. Go right here (Malham Tarn), to a stile over a wall. Immediately beyond this the path splits. Stay right and continue down to the public road.

Beyond the road, follow the path which joins the entrance drive to Malham Tarn House then turn left along this to reach a gate. Follow the clear track beyond this round the tarn as far as the house then return to the gate.

For the return route, head right from the gate, to the left of a walled wood. One of the various paths here will lead to the car park by the road.

Turn right along the road to cross Malham Water, then first left through a gate. Follow a grassy path for 100m to reach a signposted junction. Go left here (Malham Cove) and follow the path along the line of the beck to the water sinks, where the beck

disappears.

Continue along the dry valley, which becomes narrower and rockier, until the path drops over an edge and swings right to reach a stile over a wall. Cross this and turn left, down a narrow valley, to reach the top of Malham Cove.

Turn right across the limestone pavement and continue as for Walk 17 to return to Malham.

where there is a pedestrian gate. Go through this and continue with the beck beyond the boundary to your left. Cross a footbridge over a tributary beck and walk on to a gate, just beyond, with a track running through it.

Beyond the gate, the track heads off to the left. Ignore this and keep straight on across the field, parallel to the fence to your left. Pass to the right of Aire Head – the point where the River Aire bubbles up in the middle of the field – and continue to a stile in a transverse wall. Cross that and continue, with a wall to your left and the river beyond that.

When the wall cuts across your route go through a gate and continue, with the wall now on your right. The route now becomes clearer: running by the river and a mill lade down to Scalegill Mill (now flats). Pass to the right of the building to reach the metalled driveway beyond. Follow this down to join the public road at the west end of Hanlith Bridge.

Looking across to your right you will be able to see the village of Kirkby Malham and the church tower. A brief diversion along the public road leads to the village (the road is narrow, but it is quiet and visibility, over the low walls, is good). There is a splendid 15th-century church, plus the Victoria Inn.

Return to Hanlith Bridge and walk across it. Follow the road up through the village. Just beyond the last house on the left, at a hairpin bend, there is a wooden gate to the left

marked by a yellow arrow and a sign for the Pennine Way. Go through the gate, into a field.

Walk across the bottom of a narrow field, with two houses over the wall to your left, then continue across the middle of a sloping field. There is no path here, but occasional piles of stones mark the route.

A wall comes in from behind right then swings right, along the route you are following. Continue with this wall to your right to reach a gate in a transverse wall, visible ahead. Pass through this and continue along the bottom of the field beyond, with a wood to your left, to reach another transverse wall.

Go through a gate. Beyond this there is no flanking wall: just walk along the top of the steep slope dropping to your left. Aim for a kissing-gate on the far side of the field.

Beyond the gate head half-left, down the slope, towards a fragment of old wall running down the slope to the river. At the bottom of the wall there is a gap where there used to be a gate: go through that. The path is now becoming clearer.

Follow the river for 50m to reach a slab footbridge over a tributary. Cross this and continue to a kissing-gate in a fence, visible ahead. Beyond this, walk on with a field boundary to your left and a water treatment plant beyond. Head towards the right-hand end of a line of three large trees. This leads to a kissing-gate. Go through this and follow the clear path beyond back into Malham.

A steep circuit on public road, tracks and paths, wet in places, leading to a fine viewpoint. Length: **5¹/₂ miles/9km**; *Height Climbed:* **720ft/220m**. *This walk is a possible extension to Walk 16.*

O.S. Sheet OL2

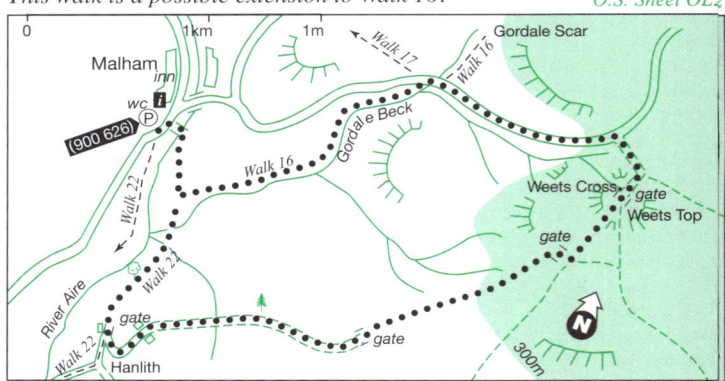

Start from the National Park car park in Malham and follow the directions for Walk 16 as far as the turn off the public road into Gordale Scar. For this route, continue climbing up the road – quieter beyond the Scar.

When the road is almost at the top of the hill a lane leads off to the right, signposted for Weets Top. Follow this lane (ignoring the stile to the left) past Weets Cross and through a gate to reach the top of the hill, from where there are spectacular views.

At this point there is a signposted junction. Go half-ahead right (signposted for Calton) on a clear track. After a short distance there is another signposted junction. This time go right (Hanlith), down to a gate in a wall. Follow the faint path through a wet, grassy moor; parallel to the

wall at first before pulling away to the right and dropping to a gate leading into a lane.

The lane drops to a group of houses and becomes a tarmac road. Continue to the first houses in the village of Hanlith where, at a hairpin bend, there is a gate on the right and a sign for the Pennine Way.

The next section is well signposted for the Pennine Way, passing through a sequence of fields above the River Aire before dropping to cross a stone slab footbridge over Gordale Beck (*see* Walk 22). Cross a stile over a fence just beyond, then pass the water treatment works and continue across the field beyond to reach a gate near a barn. This leads back on to the original path.

Turn left to return to the start.

A low-level circuit on clear tracks and rough footpaths, passing the crags by Malham Tarn and crossing rough, open grazing land. Length: **4 miles/6.5km***; Height Climbed: undulating. Possible extension to Walk 20.*

This walk can be seen either as an extension of Walk 20 or as a walk in its own right. If you have been following Walk 20, simply follow the directions given from the point where the driveway to Malham Tarn House nears the Tarn and add two miles/3km to the total distance.

If you are walking this route on its own, drive north from the village of Malham on the minor road to the west (left) of the beck. After 3 miles, turn right at a four-way junction to reach the parking area just beyond the bridge over Malham Water.

Follow one of the paths which runs north from the parking area, across the moorland, to join the driveway into the house beyond the Tarn. Follow the drive through a gate in a wall and continue until it joins the Tarn to the left. At this point there are a number of trees protected by circular walls and a track cuts back and to the right along the foot of the crags of Great Close Scar. Turn onto this.

The track swings left round the far end of the Scar and drops down to join a vehicle track. Turn left along this. As you approach Middle House Farm the track crosses a cattle grid and continues with a fence to the left. When this fence bends away from the track cut off to the left, towards a field gate in a fence, visible ahead.

O.S. Sheet OL2

Beyond the gate there is no clear path. Turn left and walk through the field, parallel to the fence to your left. Looking ahead there is a transverse fence with two gates in it. Cross the stile by the left-hand gate and continue.

The rough path climbs gently to the watershed then slants down and across the steeper slope above Malham Tarn to join the driveway just as it enters the woodland around the house.

Turn right for short distance to see the house; otherwise turn left to return to the start.

22 Malham, Kirkby Malham & Hanlith ———— B

A low-level circuit by the River Aire, passing the fine old church and inn at Kirkby Malham. Paths faint in places. Length: **3 miles/5km**; *Height Climbed:* **130ft/40m**.

O.S. Sheet OL2

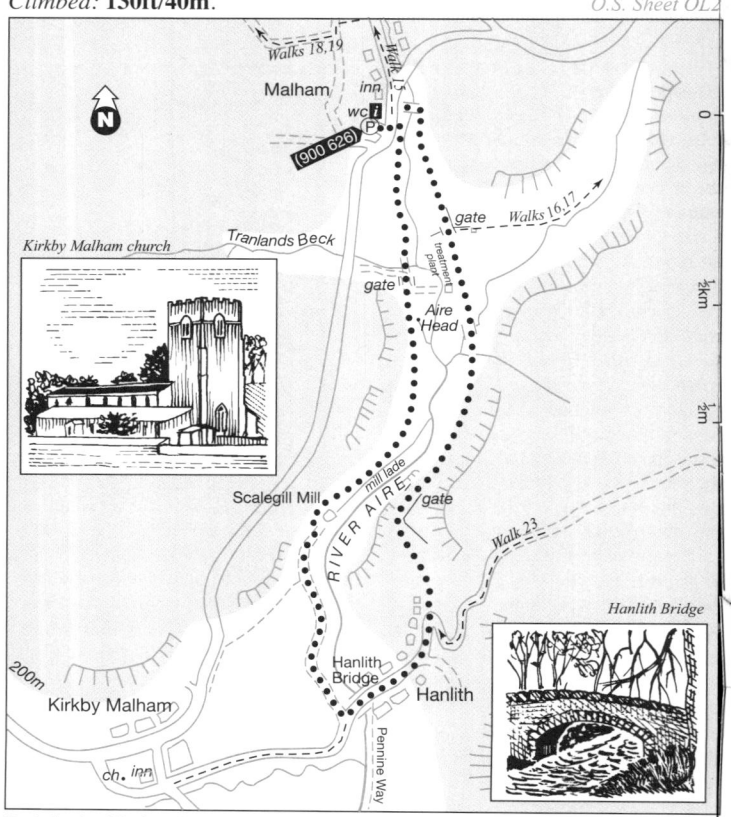

Park in the National Park car park in Malham and walk towards the village. After a short distance, level with the Methodist Chapel, there is a sign

pointing right for Hanlith Bridge.

Cross a stile and enter a field. There is no path here: walk down to the far left-hand corner of the field